SUSSEX STEAM

Scenes from the Fifties and Sixties

MICHAEL WELCH

Capital Transport

CONTENTS

First Published 1998
Reprinted 2002

ISBN 185414 202 X

Published by Capital Transport Publishing
38 Long Elmes, Harrow Weald, Middlesex

Printed by CS Graphics, Singapore

© Michael Welch 1998

Front cover: This absorbing scene at the interesting country station of Heathfield was photographed on 10th June 1965, just a few days prior to the closure of most of the Polegate to Eridge 'Cuckoo' Line to passenger traffic. The train depicted is the 1.14pm from Tunbridge Wells to Eastbourne, which is formed of a set of three Bulleid coaches hauled by BR Standard Class 4MT 2-6-4T No.80032. Heathfield stood at a height of almost 500 feet above sea level on a Wealden ridge, the station almost marking the summit of fierce climbs, mainly at a gradient of 1 in 50, in each direction. A particularly interesting feature of Heathfield station was the location of the main station building, which was constructed at right angles to the line, the booking hall being connected to the footbridge by a gallery. The station is also noteworthy for the use of natural gas for its station lighting, following the discovery of a reservoir of gas in 1896. Heathfield retained goods facilities until 26th April 1968, when the very last train ran. *J. J. Smith*

Back cover: LBSCR Class A1Xs 0–6–0T No.32635 at Brighton shed in August 1961. This little engine was built to Stroudley's design and emerged from Brighton Works in 1878 as No.35 *Morden*. In August 1946 it became the Brighton Works shunter and was renumbered in departmental service stock as 377s. The work's authorities had the inspired idea of repainting the locomotive in Stroudley yellow livery, with 'Brighton Works' lettering on its tanksides and fitting a copper capped chimney, and consequently the engine was nicknamed 'Yellow Peril' by the crews. Later it became DS 377 under the BR regime. When the works closed in the late 1950s the Terrier's status was altered and it became part of BR capital stock, being renumbered 32635. For a time the former works premises were used for the assembly of Isetta 'bubble' cars and it could sometimes be seen sprinting across the station approaches with a trainload of these brightly coloured vehicles in tow. Like the 'bubble' cars, the Terrier was also a product of Brighton works, but from a slightly earlier era! After a period in store at the back of Brighton shed in derelict condition minus its chimney, it was withdrawn in March 1963. No. 32635 was later scrapped at Eastleigh works after becoming one of the few Terriers to survive into the 1960s. *Roy Hobbs*

Overleaf: In this interesting everyday scene taken at Brighton in the early 1960s, Bulleid Light Pacific No.34057 *Biggin Hill* is seen waiting to leave Platform 2 at the head of a westbound through train. At this time, there were three steam hauled expresses along the West Coast line, the 9.40am Brighton to Bournemouth, 11am to Cardiff and 11.30am to Plymouth, and their corresponding return workings. Usually, Brighton-based Bulleid Pacifics worked these services, but despite the fact that locomotives of this type were based there for many years, Brighton shed never really mastered the intricacies of these complex machines and other types sometimes deputised when a Bulleid pacific was unavailable. Part of Brighton motive power depot is just visible on the extreme right of the picture. *Biggin Hill* was built at Brighton Works in March 1947 and remained in unrebuilt condition until withdrawal, which took place in May 1967, two months before the end of steam traction on the Southern Region. *John C. Morgan*

INTRODUCTION

Sussex is widely considered to be one of the most attractive English counties. It has a wide variety of scenery ranging from chalk downland to lush woods and forests; indeed the county is reputed to be the most heavily wooded in England. The best-known and most prominent feature of the Sussex landscape is the South Downs, stretching from north of Chichester to Beachy Head. The Sussex Weald is another delightful area where some of the county's loveliest small towns and villages can be found. Apart from the dramatic cliff scenery in the east of the county, the coastline is not spectacular and has in any case been largely spoilt by sprawling urban development along the coastal plain.

The first railway in Sussex opened in 1841 and the system was rapidly expanded by the LB&SCR, and other companies, to serve most major settlements. The diversity of the railway network which developed in the county is best illustrated by comparing the busy Brighton Line, with its heavy commuter and holiday traffic, with the sleepy single track branch line which connected Horsham with Guildford and had a meagre service of around half a dozen trains a day. Despite electrification of most of the principal routes by the Southern Railway in the 1930s, steam traction remained an everyday sight along these lines, working freight and van trains, in addition to inter-regional services. The branch lines, which were generally untouched by electrification, continued to be worked by steam traction, and a variety of pre-grouping locomotive types remained at work almost to the end of steam in the county.

In my view, the most attractive line in Sussex was the 'Cuckoo Line' which linked Eastbourne and Tunbridge Wells. This steeply-graded route traversed some of the most picturesque wealden countryside and provided one of the most enjoyable branch line journeys imaginable. Sadly, the line did not serve any significant centres of population and fell victim to the late Doctor Beeching's infamous axe in 1965.

My memories of steam trains in Sussex date from the mid-1950s when my family moved to West Worthing. At that time the star attraction along the West Coast Line through Worthing was the last-surviving LB&SCR 'Atlantic' No.32424 *Beachy Head* which often worked the Brighton to Bournemouth train. I used to watch the trains go by at Elm Grove crossing, between West Worthing and Durrington-on-Sea stations, and have vivid memories of *Beachy Head* flashing past on the return Bournemouth train at about 4.30 in the afternoon. In addition to the Bournemouth working, there were through trains from Brighton to Cardiff and Plymouth and these were usually worked by one of Brighton shed's stud of five Bulleid Light Pacifics, my particular favourite being No.34045 *Ottery St Mary*. The 'Brighton' K Class 'Moguls' also held a special place in my affections, and these locomotives, plus the E4 Class 'Large Radial' tank engines, were a familiar sight on freight workings.

During the last ten years there has been an enormous growth in the popularity of railway colour albums, but the county of Sussex has been largely overlooked and this album is designed to fill this gap. Compilation of this book has given me enormous pleasure, and rekindled many pleasant memories of those days when the railway system was infinitely more interesting than it is today. It is particularly pleasing that it has been possible to obtain a wide variety of transparencies which provide an excellent coverage of most of the lines in Sussex. Regrettably, some lines are not as well illustrated as I would have wished, while suitable slides taken between Eastbourne, Hastings and Rye have completely eluded me.

I would like to record my thanks to all the photographers who have so kindly loaned their splendid slides and made publication of this book possible. In addition, a special 'thank you' is due to Terence A Barry who scrutinised my manuscript and suggested many alterations which have vastly improved upon the original draft. Graham Mallinson also checked the manuscript and read the proofs, and thanks are also due to this gentleman.

Burgess Hill, April 1998   Michael Welch

LB&SCR K class 'Mogul' No.32345 is seen shunting in Chichester yard on 28th October 1962. Chichester station is just visible in the distance, behind the signal box. Despite still being in sound mechanical order, all the surviving members of the class were withdrawn at the end of that year and most, including 32345, were broken up at Eastleigh, but some others were eventually sold for breaking in March 1964 to R.A. King & Co at Norwich. Unfortunately no example was preserved, a sad blow for LB&SCR devotees. Chichester was the usual motive power changeover point for freight trains passing from the Western to the Central Section. Mixed-traffic locomotives such as S15 4-6-0s were the usual Western Section motive power for such trains, although on one occasion a 'Lord Nelson' 4-6-0 was seen on such a duty. Western Section engines continued to work to Chichester almost to the end of Southern Region steam in July 1967. *Mike Hudson*

THE WEST COAST LINE

Opposite top: Despite the wet conditions, Barnham station still manages to present a reasonably colourful appearance with its distinctive cream and green painted signal box, and prominent semaphore signals. The wet platform surfaces also give extra life to this picture of BR Standard Class 4MT 2-6-4T No.80019 entering the station with an unidentified eastbound working in April 1964. It is possible that it was the through Plymouth to Brighton service, for which Bulleid Pacifics were more usual motive power. This train remained regularly steam worked during the winter period, due to the shortage of electrically heated rolling stock. The tracks curving away behind the signal box are those of the short branch to Bognor Regis. The Lyminster to Chichester section of the Southern's West Coast Line, which included Barnham, was opened as a single line in June 1846, although the line was of double-track width. Today, the immediate environs of Barnham station are controlled by colour light signals, which were installed as part of the modernisation of the West Coast Line in the late 1980s. Some semaphore signals still survive on the Bognor branch, some of which are almost in sight of Barnham's signalman. *Mike Hudson*

Opposite bottom: The scene is Bognor Regis station at about 6.30am on Sunday 4th July 1965, as BR Standard Class 4MT 2-6-4T No.80083 leaves with a short train of empty newspaper vans, which it would work as far as Barnham. The vans came down from London on the 3.30am Waterloo to Portsmouth Harbour newspaper train, and were detached at Havant, before forming the 5.16am 'news' train from there to Bognor Regis. This little known working was still booked for steam traction until 17th April 1966, when Standard Class 4MT No.75077 was noted. By this time it had become one of the last (perhaps *the* last) diagrammed steam turns on the Central Division, although in fact booked for an Eastleigh-allocated locomotive. The final occasion on which steam traction was observed was on 8th May 1966, on which date No.80065 appeared. When the Portsmouth Line was blocked by engineering works, the train from Waterloo travelled via Epsom and the Mid-Sussex route, in which case the vans were detached at Barnham. *Mike Hudson*

Views of ordinary steam-hauled passenger trains at Littlehampton after electrification are rare. This shows a day excursion from Southampton to Littlehampton returning on a July weekday evening in 1963, with Eastleigh-based Standard Class 4MT No.76069 in charge. This was a typical 'bucket and spade' working for only six weeks at the height of the summer season, but this was to be its last year. When it started in the early 1950s ex-L&SWR 4-4-0s often hauled it, but later, BR Standard locomotives were the rule. After arrival at Littlehampton the engine ambled around to Bognor Regis for servicing, remaining there until about 5.15pm before returning to Littlehampton to take its train back. Presumably the engine crew spent much of the day on the beach at Bognor well away from their passengers! *Mike Hudson*

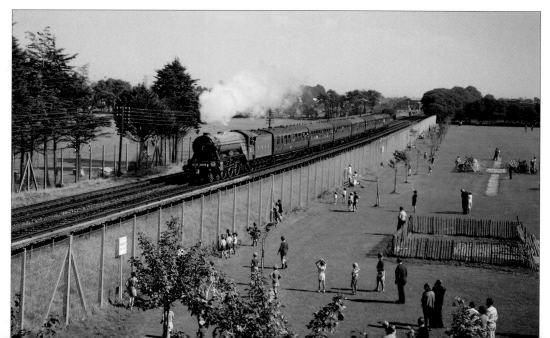

Bystanders are transfixed as ex-L&NER preserved Class A3 Pacific No.4472 *Flying Scotsman* passes West Park, between West Worthing and Durrington-on-Sea stations in September 1966. It was working a railtour from Victoria to Salisbury and return, as far as Eastleigh. It was the only occasion known to the author that this engine appeared in Sussex. The signal just visible in the background is West Worthing Up Outer Home, and beyond it can be seen the electric stock berthing shed. The picture was taken from Shaftesbury Avenue roadbridge which crosses the line immediately east of Durrington station. *John Phillips*

A very rare colour view, taken in June 1957, of SE&CR P Class 0-6-0T No.31556 shunting at Kingston Wharf, near Shoreham-by-Sea. This diminutive engine was later preserved, and can be seen on the Kent and East Sussex Railway. Since 1788 a service of cross-Channel packets had operated from here, and in 1847 the newly-formed LB&SCR decided to run its own steamers. Unfortunately, they were unable to agree terms with the harbour authorities, and decided to use Newhaven instead. Although the LB&SCR's plans for Kingston as a passenger port foundered, the prospects for goods traffic were more promising. When the railway reached Kingston in 1840, coke ovens were built to provide fuel for the engines, and a wharf was provided to permit easier loading of ships. The sidings on the wharf were connected to those on the down side of the main line by an inclined plane, which was at right angles to both sets of sidings and had a wagon turntable at each end. Wagons were hauled up by a stationary engine, and horses were used for shunting. In 1938 the system was completely remodelled. The separate basins were infilled to provide a straight quay, and the inclined plane was replaced by a tightly-curved locomotive-worked line, which descended to the wharf on a 1 in 82 gradient. This fascinating installation closed in 1968, and no trace of the railway's existence now remains. *S. C. Townroe/Colour-Rail*

When the LB&SCR moved their carriage workshops from Brighton to Lancing in 1912, the move was resented by most of the workforce, who lived in the Brighton area. The anger felt by the staff eventually boiled over into a strike, which occurred in 1919. Presumably, if the First World War had not intervened, the strike would have taken place much earlier! The strike resulted in a special train being provided for the exclusive use of the Lancing Works staff, which, in later years, left Brighton at 7.10am and returned from Lancing at 5.31pm. A highly distinctive ten or eleven-coach set of vintage coaches was provided for this working, which was known locally as the 'Lancing Belle'. The 'Belle' was generally powered by a pair of LB&SCR tank locomotives, usually E4 Class, but on occasions other types appeared. In June 1958, the train was regularly piloted by SE&CR Class D1 or L 4-4-0s. On 3rd April 1959, even more interesting motive power was recorded when 'Schools' Class 4-4-0 No.30937 *Epsom*, running tender first, piloted the evening train. No.30937 had earlier powered a stock train to Lancing, and its appearance at the head of the 'Belle' presumably saved a light engine working to Brighton. In this portrait, E4 Class No.32468, piloted by E6 Class No.32417, is seen working the evening train between Hove and Brighton stations. This was one train for which photographers preferred cloudy conditions, because the angle of the sun at that time of the evening made photography a very tricky business indeed! *Peter Hay collection*

Opposite: A commendably clean Ivatt Class 2MT 2-6-2T No.41301 is seen on a Horsham train in the early 1960s. The scene is between Brighton and Hove stations, with the portal of the New England tunnel being visible in the distance. When construction of the London to Brighton line was authorised in 1837, a stipulation was made that work on the branch to Shoreham should at least begin at the same time as work on the main line. In fact, the six miles long Shoreham branch was the first section of the London & Brighton Railway to be opened, and therefore has a considerable importance in the history of that railway. The first train to Shoreham, conveying Directors of the line and local tradesmen, left Brighton station at 3pm on Monday 11th May 1840 to the accompaniment of the National Anthem played by the band of the 12th Lancers. Regular public services commenced the following day. *Peter Hay collection*

Brighton shed's turntable occupied a very restricted space between the shed building and the boundary fence. One wonders how the residents of the adjacent road ever had a decent night's sleep, considering the noise from the shed at all hours of day and night. Here, an ex-LB&SCR K Class 'Mogul' No.32341 is being turned on 7th October 1962. The loco was built in November 1914, just a few hundred yards from this spot, at Brighton Works, and spent much of its long career based at Brighton shed. In the 1920s it was selected for trials with experimental blastpipes and sanding gear, but otherwise led an uneventful life until on 23rd April 1953 it ran into the turntable pit at its home shed, trapping ex-LB&SCR C2X Class 0-6-0 No.32434 thereon for several hours. No.32341 was reputedly the last active survivor of the class, being noted on the 7.22am Haywards Heath–Eastbourne van train on 28th December 1962. It was later scrapped at Eastleigh works. *Mike Hudson*

This view of Brighton shed, taken from platforms 1/2 was taken on a special occasion, on 7th October 1962, when the RCTS ran a 'Sussex Coast' railtour. This train, which started in London, was worked by a 'Schools' Class 4-4-0 to Brighton, from where the train proceeded to Seaford behind two LB&SCR locomotives – E6 Class 0-6-2T No.32418 piloted by 'Terrier' 0-6-0T No.32636, which are seen waiting to come 'off shed'. The railtour returned to Brighton, before returning to the Capital via Horsham and Epsom. Motive power on the latter section was provided by another 'Brighton' engine, K Class 'Mogul' No.32353. At this time, Brighton shed still retained a considerable number of LB&SCR locomotives, in addition to a fair variety of other classes, including Bulleid Pacifics and BR Standard types. By the end of 1962, most of the 'Brighton' engines (including Nos.32418 and 32353) were withdrawn, and a year later all Brighton's remaining Pacifics were transferred to other depots, as the shed's rapid run-down continued. The depot finally closed in June 1964, following the dieselisation of its last remaining steam duties. Steam traction continued to make sporadic appearances at Brighton, mainly on the through train to and from Plymouth, for almost a further two years. *Mike Hudson*

Bulleid Light Pacific No.34008 *Padstow* poses on Brighton locomotive shed's headshunt in April 1960, shortly before being called-in to Eastleigh Works for rebuilding. Brighton station's magnificent roof, which dates from the reconstruction which occurred in 1882/3, dominates the background. Part of the Brighton Works' administration offices can just be seen on the extreme left. For many years during the 1950s, Brighton shed had a regular allocation of five Bulleid Light Pacifics, but in 1958/9 they were sent away for rebuilding at Eastleigh Works, and were replaced by five other similar locomotives drafted in from various parts of the region, and these included No.34008. When *Padstow* was sent to Eastleigh to be rebuilt, it is unlikely that the Brighton shed staff expected it to return. In the event they were proved to be wrong, because *Padstow* returned to Brighton three months later, becoming the first rebuilt Bulleid Pacific to be based there.
Colour-Rail

This classic panorama of Brighton shed and other railway installations was taken on 27th October 1963. The Bluebell's locomotives, *Birch Grove* and *Stepney*, are visible in the foreground. Brighton Works is in the top right of the picture, whilst the electric stock maintenance depot can be seen above the roof of the locomotive shed. The shed was built on the site of a chalk hill which had to be removed before construction could commence. By the time this picture was taken the shed was in rapid decline, as exemplified here by the empty shed roads and preponderance of BR Standard locomotives and LM&SR – designed Ivatt Class 2MT tank engines. The shed closed the following June and the site is now occupied by a railway engineering depot.
T. B. Owen

On a bright morning in May 1964, LM&SR-designed Ivatt 2-6-2T No.41260 pulls out of Platform 1 at Brighton station with the morning Lancing Works train. The Works had been earmarked for closure in 1962 as part of a nationwide rationalisation of workshops, and by 1964 many of the workforce had already left. Consequently, the workmen's train had been slimmed down to only six coaches, and double-heading was no longer necessary. By this time, only a handful of steam locomotives, mostly Ivatt Class 2MTs and BR Standard types, remained on the books at Brighton shed, which had been reduced to a pale shadow of its former self. The end of steam traction, after over 120 years, was only a matter of weeks away. Apart from the Lancing Works train, the last remaining regular steam passenger workings in the area were those on the Steyning Line (Brighton to Horsham) service, but these were diagrammed for diesel multiple-unit operation from 4th May. The 'Lancing Belle' remained steam operated until 15th June, from which date Brighton shed was closed. From that date, the train was booked for diesel traction, but this development proved to be short-lived, because the train itself ran for the last time only a few weeks later. *G. Daniels*

THE MID-SUSSEX LINE

BR Standard Class 5MT 4-6-0 No.73021 heads south through attractive rural surroundings near Billingshurst on 29th May 1965. The engine was hauling a day excursion from Slough to Bognor Regis via Kensington Olympia and Redhill. From Bognor the engine ran light to Fratton shed for servicing before its return journey. The appearance of a steam-hauled passenger train on the Mid-Sussex line just before the complete elimination of steam traction from the Central Division was quite remarkable. After 14th June steam was officially a thing of the past in the Division, although occasional workings continued from the South Western Division. In more recent times the Mid-Sussex line has been marketed as the Arun Valley line, a geographically more appropriate title. *Mike Hudson.*

The 'Sussex Coast Limited' railtour of the Locomotive Club of Great Britain on the Mid-Sussex line *en route* to Midhurst, near Christ's Hospital on 24th June 1962. It started from Waterloo and eventually reached Eastbourne via Bognor Regis and Haywards Heath before returning to London via the 'Cuckoo Line'. One of the only three Class E6s in service, No.32417 was the train engine, piloted by E4 No.32503, one of the eight survivors of the class still in traffic. *C. Hogg*

Christ's Hospital station was opened in 1902 when the 'Bluecoat School' moved from London to spacious premises nearby. A magnificent station was constructed by the LB&SCR in order to cater for the expected heavy daily schools traffic. Unfortunately, this did not materialise because the school's governors decided that Christ's Hospital would be a boarding school, so the station became something of a white elephant. The station premises were quite commodious, with a down loop (which had platforms on both sides) being provided in addition to the two main running lines. This line was used principally by van trains unloading pupils' luggage and also by their holiday specials. Separate platforms were built to serve trains on the Guildford line. One of the Guildford tracks was also served by platforms on both sides. Tragically the station buildings were demolished by BR in the early 1970s, and the loop platform line was infilled. This photograph was taken during happier days in March 1962, when the steam worked branch lines to Brighton and Guildford were still in operation. *John Phillips*

Two LB&SCR E5X Class 0-6-2Ts, Nos.32576 and 32570, are seen at Horsham on 6th February 1955 waiting to take over the RCTS 'Hampshireman' rail tour, which was run in connection with the closure of the Pulborough to Midhurst line (and Meon Valley Line) to passenger services. Locomotives of this class were rarely photographed in colour. There were only four engines in the class, and these were all withdrawn by January 1956, before colour photography became commonplace. No.32570 was built in December 1902 and was originally named *Armington*, while its sister engine was constructed in April 1903 and named *Brenchley*. Both were built at Brighton Works as Class E5, but in 1911 they were rebuilt to Class E5X using improved C3-type boilers. These boilers were larger than those previously fitted, and various modifications to the locomotives were necessary, including raising the cabs and placing the side tanks further apart, and a more impressive design resulted. Unfortunately, although the larger boilers produced a plentiful steam supply, the locomotives still suffered from restricted steam chests, so little improvement over the E5 Class was obtained. The E5Xs spent much of their career engaged on local goods work and secondary passenger duties, with Horsham being a regular haunt of the class for many years. No.32576 was condemned just over four months after this picture was taken, while its sister engine lingered until the following January, thus acquiring the dubious distinction of being the final member of the quartet in active service. *T. B. Owen/Colour-Rail*

LB&SCR D3 Class 0-4-4T No.32390 is pictured on the turntable at Horsham shed in August 1954. This is an extremely rare, possibly unique, colour portrait of one of this class, which ceased work in 1955. No.32390 was built in May 1894 at Brighton Works to the design of Robert Billinton, for use on outer suburban and secondary passenger services. It was originally No.390 *St Leonards* and was first allocated to Brighton shed together with fourteen other members of its class. The other locomotives were based at New Cross, Battersea, Tunbridge Wells and Eastbourne sheds. During the First World War, No.390 was, most unusually, parked in a siding at Crowborough for a lengthy period supplying steam for a portable bathing unit for troops stationed in the area. In the early 1930s, all members of the class were renumbered by adding two thousand to the existing number, but some were withdrawn from service in 1933/35 as a result of spreading electrification in the London area. At that time No.2390 was based at St Leonards, working services to Ashford and Eastbourne, and in 1937 it was shedded at Tonbridge for working the through trains to Eastbourne. Many D3s were withdrawn in 1948/49, and by October 1953 No.32390 was the solitary serviceable member of its class, based at Brighton shed. It was largely employed on Brighton to Horsham trains, and other local workings, including some sorties over the 'Cuckoo' line. It was withdrawn in September 1955 with a final mileage of 1,442,773, and broken-up in Brighton Works a few months later. *S.C. Townroe/Colour-Rail*

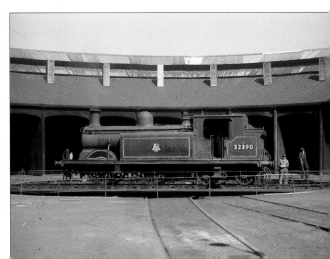

Opposite: M7 Class 0-4-4T No.30047 propels a short push-pull train of converted early L&SWR corridor stock away from Selham, on the Pulborough-Midhurst-Petersfield line, in April 1954. The station served a tiny hamlet, located at the foot of the South Downs in the valley of the River Rother, a tributary of the River Arun, which was in close proximity to the railway for some distance. The signal box here was closed in the 1930s, but the goods yard remained in use until May 1963. After the closure to passengers, the station buildings were taken over by a local farmer for the storage of agricultural equipment, and were still standing in the early 1990s. *S. C. Townroe/Colour-Rail*

Below: Maunsell Class Q 0-6-0 No.30530 is seen near Selham hauling a rail tour which formed the last passenger train from Pulborough to Midhurst on 18th October 1964. The line from Horsham to Petworth was the first route to be built in this part of Sussex and opened in 1859, before the construction of the line to the coast, which opened four years later. Midhurst was reached in October 1866 after a very protracted construction period. The route traversed a very sparsely populated rural area and agricultural traffic was the principal source of revenue. Passenger services last ran in February 1955, but goods traffic to and from Midhurst carried on until 1964. The short section from Pulborough to Petworth retained its goods service until May 1966. *G. Daniels*

Above: The Locomotive Club of Great Britain's 'Sussex Coast Limited Rail Tour' is seen at Midhurst on 24th June 1962. Two LB&SCR-designed locomotives – class E4 No.32503 and E6 No.32418 – pose for photographers prior to running around their train and returning to Pulborough. Two photographers have climbed the signal gantry behind the engines, and others have strayed off the platform. In those days there appears to have been a more relaxed official attitude towards such behaviour, and in any case there was no third rail to worry about at Midhurst! Part of Midhurst's fine LB&SCR station building, which was in surprisingly good condition, can be seen in the distance, on the left of the picture. *Mike Hudson*

Right: On a sunny spring day in 1962, a badly leaking LB&SCR Class E4 0-6-2T, No.32470, is seen shunting at Midhurst prior to departure with a freight bound for Pulborough, and presumably, Horsham. Three separate rail routes served Midhurst, the first being the line from Petersfield which was opened by the L&SWR in September 1864. The next line to reach the town was that from Pulborough which was built by the LB&SCR and opened in October 1866. The third route to enter Midhurst was probably the most interesting, both scenically and historically. This was the line from Chichester, on which construction started in 1865, but financial problems ensued, and by 1868 all work had stopped! The scheme was revived in 1876 when the LB&SCR decided to incorporate the Chichester to Midhurst line into their route from Pulborough, which involved an end-on junction with the latter, and building a new station half a mile to the east of the existing two termini! This also involved a longer walk for passengers transferring between the two companies! The line opened for business – after a very long wait – in 1881. The Chichester line was famous for the decorative architectural style of the stations, which incorporated features which can still be seen on the Bluebell Railway's stations today. When the Southern Railway took over operation of the lines in 1923, their first action was to strengthen Bepton Road bridge, the weakness of which had hitherto restricted the running of through trains between the two stations. This move enabled trains from Petersfield to run into the former LB&SCR station, and the L&SWR premises were closed. Sadly, the Chichester line's passenger workings succumbed to road competition in 1935, but the Petersfield to Pulborough line lasted much longer. Passenger services were withdrawn between the towns in February 1955. Freight trains, such as that pictured here, continued to run from the Pulborough end until the mid-1960s, while a short section of the Chichester line remained in use as far as Lavant until quite recently. *John Phillips*

HORSHAM TO GUILDFORD

On a sunny day in June 1961, LM&SR-designed Class 2MT 2-6-2T No.41301 approaches Christ's Hospital with the 10.34am Guildford to Horsham train. No.41301 was built at Crewe Works in March 1952 and was withdrawn from service in September 1966. This was a regrettably short life for an efficient little locomotive, but the traffic for which it had been designed had either ceased or had been converted to DMU operation. This train was scheduled to take 48 minutes to cover the distance of almost twenty miles, with six intermediate stops, between the two towns. The line was one of the most attractive branch lines in Sussex, but unfortunately much of the route was actually in Surrey. The county boundary crossed the line between Rudgwick and Baynards stations, so that most of the line is outside the scope of this book.
Paul Leavens

LM&SR-designed Ivatt Class 2MT 2-6-2T No.41283 enters Christ's Hospital Station with a train from Guildford to Horsham. For many years M7 Class 0-4-4Ts were the regular motive power on this line, but in 1960/61 H Class 0-4-4Ts and E4 0-6-2Ts were often seen on the route. But by the time this picture was taken, on 24th June 1962, the Ivatts were in charge of all through services. There were some short workings, from Guildford to Cranleigh, for which Guildford shed invariably turned out Q1 Class 0-6-0s. No.41283 was a widely travelled locomotive, being based in Lancashire prior to moving to the SR in 1961. It did not stay in Sussex for long, moving to Barnstaple Junction shed by the summer of 1964. *C. Hogg*

SHOREHAM TO HORSHAM

The unmistakable outline of Lancing College, and its adjacent chapel, immediately identifies the location of this picture of a Horsham to Brighton train, ambling along near Old Shoreham. The train consists of a set of three Bulleid coaches, hauled by an unidentified Ivatt 2-6-2T locomotive. The road in the foreground is that from Shoreham to Steyning, while the meandering waters of the River Adur are clearly discernible behind the train. Thus, there are three forms of transport represented in this photograph, while a fourth, air travel, from Shoreham Airport, is just out of the shot to the left! Needless to say, the river provided the first means of transport in this area. It once formed part of the Adur and Bay Bridge navigation, which allowed barges to travel inland as far as Bay Bridge, near West Grinstead. This picture was taken on 14th April 1962, a lovely spring day. *G. Daniels*

LB&SCR Class K 'Mogul' No.32345 ambles down the Horsham to Shoreham line between Bramber and Shoreham with a freight from Beeding cement works on 28th April 1962. The location of the works is marked by the belching chimney in the distance. The Steyning line was closed in March 1966, but a single track from Shoreham was retained to serve the cement works until 1980. No.32345 was one of a class of seventeen locomotives designed by Lawson Billinton and constructed at Brighton works between 1913 and 1921. It was built in December 1916 and remained in service until December 1962, when all the survivors were withdrawn. *G. Daniels*

The delightful station at Partridge Green was situated approximately half way between Shoreham and Horsham and served a small village. In this view, looking north, the goods shed, stationmaster's house and signal box are the prominent buildings. The road bridge carried the Steyning to Horsham road across the railway. This portrait was taken during the summer of 1963. Although the station was quite well-sited, the village was small, and shoppers for Steyning, Horsham or Brighton all found that the local bus took them nearer to the shops. Perhaps it was a case of unfair competition! *G. Daniels*

Left: LM&SR-designed Ivatt Class 2MT 2-6-2T No.41314 leaves Southwater on a bright afternoon with the 3.59pm Brighton to Horsham train, which is formed of a three-coach set of comfortable Bulleid coaches. This photograph was taken in the spring of 1964 shortly before the introduction of diesel-electric multiple units on this route. When the line was built, part of the cottage (on the right) was found to be obstructing the route and a corner of the building was removed, thus creating an architectural curiosity. Needless to say the cottage has outlived the railway! *G. Daniels*

Above: This scene was photographed in March 1962 at Itchingfield Junction, just south of Christ's Hospital station, where the Steyning route diverged from the Mid-Sussex Line. Railway workers continue at work on the main line tracks, apparently installing point rodding, as an Ivatt Class 2MT 2-6-2T takes the Steyning Line with a Horsham to Brighton train. The train comprises a two-coach push-pull set, converted from Maunsell main line stock, plus an unidentified coach at the rear. It should be noted however that push-pull working on this route had ceased by this time, because the Ivatt locomotives were not fitted for this type of operation. The playing fields of the famous Christ's Hospital public school are on the right of the picture. The Horsham to Brighton trains remained steam operated until May 1964, when diesel units took over. *John Phillips*

THE BRIGHTON LINE

Brighton station's impressive overall roof is a familiar landmark for rail travellers, but very few are likely to have admired the superb structure from the viewpoint seen here. At the time, the photographer was employed as a carpenter engaged on roof repairs, and the opportunity to capture absorbing scenes such as this on film was presumably one of the unofficial perks of the job. This superb and fascinating shot was taken on 20th May 1965, shortly before the elimination of steam working on the Central Division. It shows BR Standard Class 4MT 2-6-4T No.80142 at the buffer stops in Platform 7 with a van train, which contains some passenger stock in its formation. Actually, the steam engine appears to be one of the more modern items of equipment visible. The electric units date from the 1930s, while the telephone booths and the water bowser do not seem to be much younger! The station roof, platforms and LB&SCR clock are still very much the same today, but all the buildings beyond the platform ends have been swept away, the locomotive works (on the right) being demolished in 1969. *J. H. W. Kent*

In this rare colour view of a 'King Arthur' N15 Class 4-6-0 at Brighton, No.30796 *Sir Dodinas le Savage* is seen leaving the Sussex resort with the RCTS 'Sussex Coast Limited' railtour on 13th April 1958, which was run to mark the withdrawal of the last 'Brighton' Atlantic, No.32424 *Beachy Head*. The building on the left is Brighton Locomotive Works. Note the train's colourful formation, which includes vehicles in three distinct liveries. The first vehicle, in green livery, is a Maunsell-designed coach from the late 1920s, while most of the other vehicles are immaculate, possibly brand new, BR Standard Mk.1 carriages, which are in carmine and cream colours. The fourth coach is Pullman Car *Myrtle*, which is in traditional Pullman livery. On the right one of the Southern Railway's '6-PUL' six-car electric units can be discerned in an adjacent platform, probably waiting to leave on a fast working to Victoria. These units were built by the Southern Railway in 1932 for the electrification of the Brighton Line. *R. C. Riley*

Left: A Northampton to Brighton day excursion, hauled by LM&SR Class 5MT 4-6-0 No.45349, passes Lovers Walk, between Preston Park and Brighton stations, on 31st May 1964. Two of the access tracks to Lovers Walk depot are visible on the left of the picture. The carriage washing machine is located on the westernmost line. In the left background can be seen the Preston Park Pullman shops, with one of the famous 'Brighton Belle' units berthed alongside. The Pullman works, which had been on this site since 1928, closed in January 1964, but the buildings still stand at the time of writing. Brighton has been a popular resort since the days of the Prince Regent. The development of Brighton was hastened by the coming of the railway in 1841, and by the turn of the century there were thirty trains from the Capital each weekday, though it is likely that some of these were slow trains not used by through London passengers. The 1950s saw a considerable expansion of inter-regional holiday traffic, particularly at weekends, and for a time there was a regular through working for a LM&SR Class 5MT on a holiday train from Manchester. In August 1953, it was recorded that no fewer than thirteen through trains to the Midlands and North of England were booked to leave the Sussex coast on one day. Day excursion traffic was also buoyant, and 'Black Five' locomotives continued to visit Brighton, and other Sussex coast resorts, regularly until about 1964. These locomotives normally monopolised the inter-regional workings, but on occasions unusual classes appeared. On 8th August 1953, for example, a LM&SR 'Jubilee' 4-6-0 No.45595 *Southern Rhodesia* was an unprecedented sight at the Sussex resort when it worked through on a train from Manchester. Another stranger was Class 4F 0-6-0 No.44043, which powered an excursion from Luton to Brighton on 31st July 1958. Today, most visitors prefer to travel by car – such is progress! *Mike Hudson*

Right: LB&SCR K Class 'Mogul' No.32353 heads the LCGB 'Sussex Coast Limited' railtour away from the 492 yards long Patcham Tunnel on 24th June 1962. No.32353 worked the train from Bognor Regis to Haywards Heath, where the preserved T9 Class locomotive No.120 took over for the next stage of the tour. The splendid condition of No.32353 was not superficial, because this machine was one of the three members of the class which received a general repair at Eastleigh Works during 1961. Sadly, just over six months later all the surviving K class engines were withdrawn as part of an accountancy move designed to reduce the number of steam locomotives inherited by the British Railways Board. *C. Hogg*

The visit of the beautiful Caledonian Railway Single locomotive No.123 was one of the most memorable occasions in the more recent history of the Brighton Line. On 15th September 1963, No.123 piloted L&SWR T9 Class 4-4-0 No.120 on a Victoria to Sheffield Park rail tour, organised by the Bluebell Railway, as far as Haywards Heath, from where both engines proceeded to Brighton for servicing. The locomotives are pictured here approaching Keymer Junction *en route* to Brighton, with Wivelsfield station in the distance. After being 'turned, coaled and watered' they travelled to Horsted Keynes, where they attracted a crowd of about 2,000 admirers. Later the two engines returned the excursionists to London, a top speed of 68mph being achieved twice during the journey. No.123 was constructed by Neilson & Co. of Glasgow in 1886, and ran in ordinary service until 1935. After the war it was partially restored and made occasional appearances at various events as a static locomotive, but in 1958 the Scottish Region made the inspired decision to restore it to working order and to Caledonian Railway livery, for use on special trains. Unfortunately it is not currently operational. *John C. Morgan*

Prior to the closure of the Ardingly branch in October 1963, the Bluebell Railway organised a number of railtours which usually originated in London, and transferred to Bluebell metals at Horsted Keynes, before proceeding to Sheffield Park. On 31st March 1963, a special train from Victoria was powered by the Bluebell's LB&SCR Class E4 0-6-2T No.473 *Birch Grove*, piloted by BR Standard 2-6-4T No. 80084. On arrival at Haywards Heath, No.80084 was detached and proceeded to Brighton shed for servicing, while *Birch Grove* remained on the train. The Bluebell's L&SWR Adams 'Radial' tank locomotive No.488 was attached at the other end, and the formation then set off to Horsted Keynes with the 'Adams' at the front and *Birch Grove* on the rear. Later in the day, No.80084 returned with its train from Haywards Heath to London single-handed, and is seen here making an energetic start away from Haywards Heath, as it crosses from the down loop platform to the up fast line. *John Phillips*

On 17th September 1966, L&NER Pacific No.4472, *Flying Scotsman*, arguably the most famous steam locomotive of all time, visited the Brighton Line. It powered a railtour from Victoria to Salisbury as far as Eastleigh. The train is pictured passing Copyhold Junction, just north of Haywards Heath, *en route* to Brighton. On arrival at Brighton station a large crowd greeted the arrival of *Flying Scotsman*, which was making its first visit to the town. The line on the right of the picture was the former Horsted Keynes branch which had been closed to passenger services in October 1963. By this time only a single track remained to serve a stone terminal at Ardingly. *N.W. Sprinks*

The Ouse Valley viaduct, located on the Brighton Line north of Haywards Heath, is one of the best-known railway landmarks in Sussex and a masterpiece of Victorian engineering; it has 37 arches and is 1,475 feet long. It was built in 1840/41, using materials which were brought up the River Ouse by barge. Eleven million bricks are reputed to have been used in its construction. Among the structure's most interesting features are the sets of 'temples' or 'pavilions' at each end. The contract price for this magnificent viaduct was just £38,500! In this picture a return Victoria to Sheffield Park railtour, hauled by BR Standard 2-6-4T No.80084, is seen crossing the viaduct on 31st March 1963. *G. Daniels*

THE KEMP TOWN BRANCH

In this rarely photographed scene, E4 Class 0-6-2T No.32503 heads the daily goods train from Brighton to Kemp Town past the site of the former Hartington Road Halt, on 17th March 1961. The halt was built of wood and was only open from January 1906 to April 1911, so it is hardly surprising that no trace remains. Two viaducts are partially visible in the picture, the longer of which is the fourteen-arch Lewes Road viaduct (in the middle background), while the train has just passed over the three-arch Hartington Road viaduct: the rooftops of Brighton form the backdrop. The Kemp Town branch, which opened on 2nd August 1869, was built to serve the rapidly growing residential area to the east of Brighton. It diverged from the Lewes line soon after leaving London Road station, and involved heavy engineering works. In addition to the viaducts mentioned above, there was also Kemp Town tunnel (1,024 yards). It was, however, a circuitous route and later suffered competition from a direct and frequent tram service, despite the very generous train service provided. The branch was closed to passenger traffic on 1st January 1933, the first day of the Brighton main line electrification scheme, but remained open for freight until 1971. *G. Daniels*

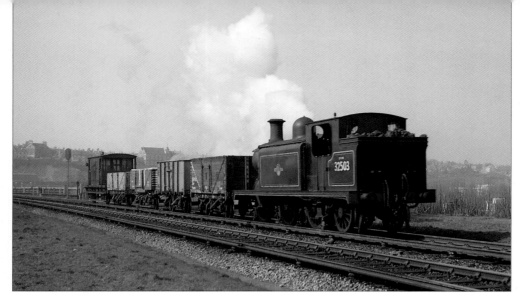

The LB&SCR E4 Class 0-6-2T locomotives were designed by Robert Billinton and first introduced in 1897 for secondary passenger and goods work. It was a successful design and a total of seventy-five were built at Brighton Works in various batches, the last example emerging in September 1903. No.32503, seen here approaching London Road (Brighton) station with a freight for Kemp Town, was constructed in August 1900 and originally named *Buckland*. These engines were an everyday sight at Brighton for more than sixty years and No.32503 was the penultimate member of its class active in the Brighton area, surviving until April 1963. *G. Daniels*

THE EAST COAST LINE

LM&SR-designed Ivatt Class 2MT 2-6-2T No.41261 passes through London Road station, between Brighton and Falmer, with a freight train from Kemp Town on Christmas Eve 1962. Note the attractive station furniture consisting of platform canopies, green painted station signs and gas lamps, all of which have long since disappeared. Ditchling Road tunnel is visible in the background. No doubt mindful of the fact that most of the remaining LB&SCR locomotives were facing withdrawal within a few days, the photographer was hoping that a Class E4 locomotive would be working this train, but, alas, on this occasion he was disappointed. *Mike Hudson*

Kemp Town Junction, situated just over a mile outside Brighton station on the Lewes line, provided an interesting and well-balanced photographic spot. In this view 'Schools' Class 4-4-0 No.30904, *Lancing*, has just emerged from the 63-yards long Ditchling Road tunnel and passes Kemp Town Junction signal box with an inter-regional relief train to Hastings, which is mainly composed of LM&SR rolling stock. This photograph was taken on 1st July 1961.
G. Daniels

Trains from Brighton to Lewes faced the formidable climb of Falmer Bank, which consisted of nearly four miles of gradients ranging from 1 in 258 to 1 in 101. In the opposite direction it was much worse, the gradient being 1 in 88! In this view 'Schools' Class 4-4-0 No.30934, *St Lawrence* is seen descending the bank, between Falmer and Lewes, with a train from Brighton to Tonbridge on 1st July 1961. The locomotive's wide chimney indicates that it was fitted with a Lemaître blastpipe, which was a modification carried out in May 1940. No.30934 was badly damaged in an air raid at Cannon Street station on 11th May 1941, when a bomb hit the locomotive's cab and pierced the firebox. It was later towed to Eastleigh Works where a spare boiler was fitted and *St Lawrence* returned to traffic in August 1941. This picture was taken when No.30934 was based at Tonbridge shed for working the Brighton trains.
G. Daniels

A historic and sad moment at Lewes on 13th April 1958, as the last surviving LB&SCR H2 Class Atlantic No.32424 *Beachy Head* approaches the station for the last time *en route* to Brighton after working the 'Sussex Coast Limited' railtour from Victoria to Newhaven Harbour. The tour was run to commemorate the end of the 'Brighton' Atlantics, No.32424 being withdrawn from service almost immediately afterwards. The class was associated with the operation of the Newhaven boat trains for many years, so *Beachy Head* was on familiar territory. The tour, which consisted of seven coaches including Pullman Car *Myrtle*, left Victoria at 10.25am and during the journey the Atlantic achieved a maximum speed of 70mph crossing the Ouse Valley viaduct. After arrival at Newhaven Harbour the train was hauled to Newhaven Town station by 'Terrier' No.32640. BR Standard 2-6-4T No.80154, the last locomotive to be built at Brighton Works, later hauled the special to Brighton, where preserved L&SWR 4-4-0 No.563 and 'Terrier' No.82 *Boxhill* were on display at the shed. Sadly, *Beachy Head* was not destined to share their good fortune in preservation. On 24th April it worked an empty stock train from Lancing Works to Micheldever from where it 'retired' to Eastleigh Works where it was cut-up for scrap within a few weeks – a tragic end to a superb class. *R. C. Riley*

The South Downs and distant rooftops of Lewes provide a superb backdrop to this fine picture of Bulleid 'West Country' Pacific No.34108, *Wincanton*, as it crosses the River Ouse at Southerham Junction with a railtour bound for Eastbourne on 19th March 1967. On the outward journey the special ran via Brighton, but on the return trip a direct non-stop run via Plumpton was made. *Wincanton* was pressed into service at short notice due to the failure of the booked locomotive at Nine Elms shed the previous evening, consequently it was not in the sparkling external condition normally expected of railtour engines. It was built at Brighton Works in April 1950, rebuilt at Eastleigh in May 1961 and withdrawn for scrap in June 1967. This train is understood to have been the final steam working in the County of Sussex before steam traction was eliminated from the Southern Region in July 1967. *G. Daniels*

During the autumn of 1960 the south of England experienced very heavy rainfall, and this flooded a lot of low lying land. The Lewes area was particularly badly affected, and the situation became so bad that Lewes station had to be partially closed. It was not possible for electric traction to use any part of the station and those services that operated were steam worked. Services on most routes were abandoned from 3rd November until about mid-morning on 6th November, but steam trains continued to run from Brighton to Eastbourne, operating on an improvised timetable. Lewes Bonfire celebrations that year must have been the soggiest ever! One of the most remarkable sights during the emergency was that of a Lewes signalman rowing out to his post on the morning of Friday 4th November. Any locomotive that could turn a wheel was pressed into service, and in this view SE&CR C Class 0-6-0 No.31686 is seen approaching Southerham Junction with the 11.12am Brighton to Eastbourne train on 5th November. Use of these engines on passenger work was commonplace on their home territory, but the sight of one shuffling along on an East Coast line passenger working was quite unprecedented. Note the submerged fields on the right, adjacent to the River Ouse, the course of which is almost lost in the great flood. *J. J. Smith*

In the early 1960s there was still a thriving inter-regional holiday traffic between the various industrial centres in the Midlands and North and the South Coast. The 1960 timetable advertised six summer Saturday workings to Hastings and Eastbourne from such diverse cities as Birmingham, Leicester, Sheffield and Manchester. In reality, many relief trains were also provided in addition to the booked services and unbalanced workings often resulted, which meant that rolling stock often had to be worked back empty to its owning region. One such working is seen here, the 9.40am special empties from Eastbourne to Willesden, which is depicted between Hampden Park and Polegate on 29th July 1961. Motive power was provided by 'West Country' Class Pacific No.34100, *Appledore*. The polished condition of the locomotive will be noted: it had worked the last down steam hauled 'Golden Arrow' some weeks previously, for which it was specially cleaned, and efforts were obviously being made to maintain it in exemplary condition. *J. J. Smith*

A rather unkempt BR Standard Class 4 2-6-4T No.80084, stands at what remains of Eastbourne shed on 13th June 1965. For many years Eastbourne depot was a sub-shed of Brighton, but when the latter closed in June 1964, Eastbourne shed became the principal servicing point for steam traction in East Sussex, although in reality it is likely that only the most basic attention could be given to defective locomotives. The dirty condition of the locomotive was all too common in the last years of steam. This photograph was taken on the last day of operation of steam traction on the Central Division. On 14th June 1965 steam traction officially became a thing of the past on the division, although occasional workings continued for some months after. *Floreat Vapor!*
J. J. Smith

THE SEAFORD BRANCH

Newhaven Town station's impressive LB&SCR signal box and wide level crossing gates are prominent in this view of LB&SCR 'Terrier' No.32636 and E6 Class No.32418 approaching the station with an RCTS rail tour, on 7th October 1962. The non-electrified line on the left of the picture provided access to the locomotive shed, which was located behind the photographer. The connection to the West Quay line can also be seen, on the left, beyond the crossing. In contrast to the veteran locomotives, the train is made up of modern BR Standard stock. The railway reached Newhaven in December 1847, when the branch from Lewes was opened, and a single line extension to Seaford was brought into use in June 1864. The Newhaven to Seaford section was converted to double track in 1904, but has since reverted to single line status. *R. C. Riley*

For obvious reasons, transparencies of locomotives in pre-nationalisation livery are scarce, so it was particularly pleasing to trace this beautiful shot of LB&SCR Atlantic No.2425 *Trevose Head*, which was taken at Newhaven shed in June 1949. No.2425 was one of six 'Brighton' Atlantics built at Brighton Works in 1911/12 to the design of Douglas Earle Marsh. In LB&SCR days it was numbered 425, and on entering traffic was allocated to Brighton shed for use on the prestigious London services. In 1926 No.2425 was named *Trevose Head* as a result of an initiative by the Southern Railway's publicity department. Unfortunately, the naming coincided with some decline in status due to the introduction of 'King Arthur' Class 4-6-0s on the Brighton Line. In the 1930s, No.2425 spent some time based at Bognor Regis shed for working London expresses both via the Mid-Sussex route and Worthing. Following electrification of the Mid-Sussex Line in 1938, other work had to be found for the Atlantics, which were still in good condition, and they spent most of the early 1940s on the Western and Eastern sections. In 1946, however, *Trevose Head* received a general overhaul at Eastleigh Works which included a repaint into malachite green livery, in which it is seen here. In the following years No.2425 found regular employment working secondary passenger and van trains on the Brighton and Uckfield lines, in addition to appearances on the Newhaven boat trains. During the early 1950s, *Trevose Head* spent long periods in store, although it was kept busy during the summer months working inter-regional holiday trains, and often powered the Brighton to Bournemouth through train. *Trevose Head* survived until September 1956, being finally withdrawn due to cracked framing and badly worn cylinders.
W. H. G. Boot/Colour-Rail

In a picture full of absorbing interest, Newhaven shed yard is seen on 7th October 1962. Apart from the turntable and the whitewashed wall of the turntable pit, the two locomotives are the most prominent subjects on view in the foreground. They are LB&SCR E4 Class No.32503, nearest the camera, and diminutive 'Terrier' 0-6-0T No.32670. The last E4 left Newhaven about six months after this picture was taken, while the 'Terriers' lasted until the following August. Note the coal stage and typical 'Brighton' water crane, both of which help to give the scene such a neat appearance. In the middle background a wooden footbridge links the main road with the up platform of Newhaven Town station, which is partially visible on the extreme right. The crossing gates can also be discerned, together with the adjacent signal box. Beyond the urban development within the town's immediate environs, the South Downs rise to a height of over 600ft. *R. C. Riley*

No doubt to the intense frustration of motorists, traffic on the main A259 Brighton to Eastbourne road is briefly halted as Terrier No.32670 takes a train of engineer's wagons from the West Quay line across the swing bridge at Newhaven on a dull day in May 1962. Originally built in December 1872 as No.70 *Poplar* this locomotive was almost 90 years old at the time of this picture. It had been withdrawn by the LBSCR in 1901 and sold to the Rother Valley Railway, later the Kent & East Sussex Railway (K&ESR), becoming their No.3 *Bodiam*. It was taken into BR stock in 1948, so never worked for the Southern Railway. After stints working at Dover and on loan to Kemsley paper mill, near Sittingbourne, it moved to Brighton in 1958 for local duties which included various turns at Newhaven. It finished its eventful career on the Havant to Hayling Island service and was withdrawn when that line was closed in November 1963. Upon withdrawal it was saved for preservation on the K&ESR where it remains today. *Roy Hobbs*

When the Lewes to Newhaven branch opened to passengers on 8th December 1847 it was confidently expected that Newhaven would become a great port, the 'Liverpool of the South', according to a guide book of 1852. But sailings depended on the tides, and it was clear that if the port was to develop, work would have to be undertaken to make it non-tidal. In the 1870s the Newhaven Harbour Company and LB&SCR decided on a massive improvement scheme, which included extensive dredging of the harbour and construction of a long mole on the western side of the river mouth. To assist in the construction of the mole the West Quay Tramway was built, in about 1879. In addition, the branch served the harbourmaster's stores, a rope works and a tarpaulin factory. It was lightly laid and only Class A1X 'Terriers' were permitted on the tramway. The most famous of these was No.32636, formerly No.72, *Fenchurch*, which was sold to the Newhaven Harbour Company in 1898 and was very much part of the Newhaven scene until it was transferred away in 1955. The task of working the last trains on the tramway fell to sister engine No.32678 however, and this is seen shunting near the harbourmaster's storeshed in August 1963, shortly before closure. *G. Daniels*

Opposite: The line from Lewes to Seaford takes advantage of a gap in the South Downs through which runs the River Ouse. In this quite rare colour picture of a steam train in action on the Seaford branch, 'Battle of Britain' Class Pacific No.34089, *602 Squadron*, is seen nearing Southerham Junction with the 6.40pm Newhaven Harbour to Victoria boat train on 10th June 1962. *J. J. Smith*

LEWES TO EAST GRINSTEAD

Few stations in Sussex have had such an interesting and eventful history as Horsted Keynes. The station was located on the Lewes to East Grinstead line and opened on 1st August 1882, becoming a junction when the branch from Haywards Heath opened for traffic just over a year later. A large, well-appointed station was provided, miles from any potential source of passenger traffic, apart from the small village of Horsted Keynes, which was just over a mile away. On 7th July 1935, the branch from Haywards Heath was electrified, and at that time it was anticipated that all the route to Croydon (via East Grinstead and Oxted) would be similarly treated, but the Second World War intervened. *J. J. Smith*

The location of this photograph will be recognised immediately by many readers, Horsted Keynes station on the Bluebell Railway. It depicts a one-coach Lewes to East Grinstead train leaving behind BR Standard Class 4MT tank locomotive No.80154, on an unknown date in 1957. The passenger service between those towns had been withdrawn when the line was closed in June 1955. The closure had provoked many protests, and one of the objectors, a Miss Bessemer of Chailey, subsequently discovered that the closure had been illegal. It transpired that this could only be effected by Parliamentary authority, and not by the independent action of the railway company. So, with considerable loss of face BR was forced to reopen the line in August 1956, and to provide the minimum service stipulated in the original Act of Parliament authorising the line. The 'sulky service', as it became known, operated only for a limited period during the middle of the day, and did not serve certain stations on the line which were not mentioned in the Act. The line was finally closed in March 1958, after the necessary legalities had been completed. As is well known, however, that was not the end of the story, because the Bluebell Railway took over a section of the line. It currently operates from Sheffield Park to Kingscote, and is actively planning to extend the operation through to East Grinstead. *N. W. Sprinks*

Another picture of a northbound departure from Horsted Keynes shows K Class 2-6-0 No.32343 leaving at the head of the 3.28pm Haywards Heath to London Bridge train on 30th April 1955. Leamland bridge is partially visible on the left of the photograph. This train later formed a rush hour return working for homegoing commuters, and was, by the standards of other trains serving the Horsted Keynes to East Grinstead line, a heavy formation. It usually comprised a 3-coach SE&CR 'Birdcage' set, a 3-coach Bulleid set and a loose vehicle coupled at the rear. While electric trains provided a fast, if rather soulless, service from Haywards Heath to London, the 3.28pm offered a more leisurely alternative for the afficionado! In addition to its interesting formation, the train was also remarkable for its unpredictable motive power. For example, during its last month of operation, Maunsell N and U1 Class 'Moguls' were noted, in addition to the more usual LB&SCR K Class engines. *R. C. Riley*

THREE BRIDGES TO TUNBRIDGE WELLS

The timeless branch connection scenario, with SE&CR H Class 0-4-4T No.31551 resting at Three Bridges shortly after arrival with a train from East Grinstead. The train, formed of a pair of Maunsell coaches converted for push-pull working, stands under the overall roof of the down bay platform. Push-pull operation of this service lasted until 4th January 1964, from which date the surviving H Class tank engines, including No.31551, were withdrawn. The buildings on this side of the station dated back to the earliest days of the Brighton Line, but they were sadly demolished in the early 1980s. Three Bridges area signalling centre and a warehouse were subsequently built on the site, when the passenger facilities on this side of the station were reduced to the barest essentials. *G. Daniels*

Rowfant Station was primarily built for the local landowner, Curtis Miranda Lampson, who, in return for making available the land through which the railway ran, was provided with this very distinctive station. One of the features of the ornamented building was an alcove, visible behind the platform lamp, which enabled his coachman to shelter from the elements. There was a brickworks on the up side, approaching the station from the east, which was served by its own private siding. A loop line, footbridge (later removed) and up platform were added at the turn of the century. *G. Daniels*

Left: An immaculate ex-works SE&CR H Class 0-4-4T No.31530 is a joy to behold, as it pauses in the attractive surroundings of Rowfant station with a train from Three Bridges to East Grinstead, in February 1960. The coaches forming the train are some of the few-remaining vehicles of SE&CR origin, which were soon to be replaced by the conversions from Maunsell stock. *John Phillips*

Above: H Class 0-4-4T No.31263 seems to be in rather a hurry to return to Tunbridge Wells shed – perhaps, in railway parlance, it was a 'going home turn' for the crew! This locomotive still survives today, superbly restored as SE&CR No.263 at the Bluebell Railway. Following withdrawal from BR service it was purchased by the H Class Locomotive Trust and stored in the open at Robertsbridge where a start was made on restoration. Later No.31263 was moved to the former South Eastern Steam Centre at Ashford, Kent, where members of the Trust undertook a complete boiler overhaul. The Trust's members later decided to move the engine to the Bluebell Railway, which offered more scope for running, and it eventually arrived at Sheffield Park in January 1976. *J. J. Smith*

Above: A train from Three Bridges runs into East Grinstead (High Level) station in early 1963. The first station to be constructed at East Grinstead was the terminus of the branch from Three Bridges, opened in 1855, which was the first railway to reach the town. The second station opened in 1866 when the line was extended to Tunbridge Wells. A third was built, on a different site, when the route from Lewes reached East Grinstead in 1882. This was constructed on two levels, the former low level platforms being used by trains on the Lewes line, as well as some terminating London trains. Following closure of the Three Bridges to Tunbridge Wells section in 1967, the high level platforms were removed and part of the course of the line eastwards was converted into a road. *G. Daniels*

Right: Class H No. 31551 is seen working the 11.08am from Three Bridges to Tunbridge Wells West on 9th June 1963, a rather hazy summer's day. The train, which was pictured between Rowfant and Grange Road stations, was comprised of push and pull set No.619, which was converted from orthodox Maunsell locomotive-hauled stock in 1960. The vehicle visible is an open third coach, dating from 1930. *J. J. Smith*

On 22nd March 1964, the RCTS/LCGB sponsored a rail tour which traversed some of the Sussex branch lines which were threatened with closure. The train started from Waterloo behind Q1 Class No.33027 and ran down to Guildford via West Clandon, before proceeding to Cranleigh and Horsham. On arrival at Horsham the train reversed, with N Class 'Mogul' No.31411 taking over for the run down the Steyning line, along the coast to Hove, and up the Brighton Line as far as Three Bridges. The tour then headed in an easterly direction to Tunbridge Wells West, with the Q1 again in charge. The participants were then treated to a run over the scenic 'Cuckoo' line behind 'Battle of Britain' Class Pacific No.34066 *Spitfire*, and eventually Pevensey was reached, where the train reversed. No.31411 took over control again, the train's next scheduled halt being made in the interesting surroundings of Lewes old station, after which the special proceeded to Brighton. A trip over the Kemp Town branch then followed, before a return was made to London via Uckfield. During the run back to London *Spitfire* was once again in charge, and a maximum speed of 73 mph was reached near Edenbridge. In this picture, the train is depicted leaving East Grinstead (High Level) station *en route* to Tunbridge Wells. On the left, the goods only line down to the Low Level goods yard is clearly visible. *D. H. Ballantyne*

BR Standard Class 4MT tank locomotive No.80140 pauses at Hartfield Station between East Grinstead and Tunbridge Wells, with a long train presumably *en route* from Tunbridge Wells to London. At this point the railway runs along the upper Medway valley, the river itself being hidden from view by the trees on the left of the picture.
G. Daniels

59

LEWES TO TUNBRIDGE WELLS

The whole of the line from Hurst Green, south of Oxted, to Lewes was tabled for closure in the Beeching Report, but local opposition saved the route north of Uckfield which remains a vital link for commuters. This picture of Barcombe Mills station was taken shortly before closure took place, the light sprinkling of snow and clear blue sky adding interest to the scene. *G. Daniels*

A sign at the former Barcombe Mills station on the Eridge to Lewes line. Is any further explanation necessary? The station, originally opened as Barcombe, closed for goods working on 6th May 1963, but passenger trains lasted until a premature closure (due to the condition of the viaduct at Lewes) on 24th February 1969. A railway replacement bus service served the station until 4th May 1969, when final closure occurred. *G. Daniels*

A rural scene . . . this was the view from the southern end of the southbound platform at Barcombe Mills Station in February 1969. Note that the station had at least been equipped with BR totems. *G. Daniels*

The sun appears to have popped out of an otherwise cloudy sky at just the right moment (or did the photographer patiently wait for it to appear?) and beautifully illuminates Maunsell Q Class 0-6-0 No.30549 as it shunts at Barcombe Mills station on 17th February 1961. The two youngsters on the platform appear to be fascinated by the antics of the photographer! No.30549 was built at Eastleigh Works in September 1939, the last of a class of twenty engines to be constructed. It sports a BR Class 4 plain blastpipe and hideous stovepipe chimney which were fitted in 1955, the result of draughting and steaming trials carried out at Swindon. No.30549 was, however, one of the first of its class to be withdrawn, which occurred in July 1963. *G. Daniels*

On the beautiful evening of 8th June 1962, 'West Country' Class Pacific No.34008, *Padstow*, is seen hauling the 4.40pm London Bridge to Brighton train. The picture was taken just south of Redgate Mill Junction, between Eridge and Crowborough, where the 'Cuckoo Line' diverged from the 'main line' to Lewes and Brighton. No.34008 achieved a small entry in the history books when it became the first rebuilt Bulleid Pacific to be allocated to Brighton shed, in November 1960. The train is made up of Bulleid and Maunsell-designed vehicles. This rural line is still open as far as Uckfield, mainly for the benefit of commuters, but the section southwards to Lewes closed in 1969. *J. J. Smith*

Above: Steam in the landscape! In this view, an unidentified SE&CR L Class 4-4-0 is seen hauling a Tonbridge to Brighton train between Eridge and Redgate Mill Junction in 1957. Redgate Mill Junction was the point of divergence between the Polegate and Lewes lines. A truly delightful Wealden scene, which could still be photographed today, but now, alas, with only an uninspiring and lifeless diesel unit, rather that this lively steam train. *N. W. Sprinks*

Right: Viewed from the verandah of the signal box, BR Standard Class 4 2-6-4T No.80138 is seen passing Birchden Junction, just north of Eridge, with the 12.32pm from Tunbridge Wells West to Brighton on 22nd July 1961. Birchden Junction signal box, which stood in a tranquil setting surrounded by pleasant countryside, controlled the divergence of the lines to Oxted (left) and Tunbridge Wells (right). The passenger train service from London/Oxted to Uckfield still runs this way, albeit on a single line, but the line to Tunbridge Wells is no more, having succumbed to closure in 1985. A preservation society has reopened a section of the latter route, and has already acquired a considerable amount of rolling stock. *John Phillips*

LM&SR-designed Fairburn Class 4MT 2-6-4T No.42103 is seen just south of Groombridge Junction with the 6.39pm Tunbridge Wells West to Eastbourne train on 15th June 1957. A batch of 41 of these competent machines was built at Brighton Works in the early 1950s to replace the remaining LB&SCR passenger locomotives, many of which were in very poor condition following years of wartime neglect. No.42103 entered service in September 1950 and worked on the Southern Region until December 1959, when it was transferred to the London Midland Region. It lasted in service until May 1965, a tragically short working life. The coaching stock is in carmine and cream livery, which makes a change from the familiar SR green! *C. Hogg*

On a sunny September day in 1959, LB&SCR K Class 'Mogul' No.32343 was photographed approaching Groombridge with the 11.53am freight train from Tunbridge Wells West to Lewes. There are four of the distinctive Southern Railway-designed vans included in the formation, which tend to give it the appearance of a van train! On the right of the picture, Groombridge's home signals indicate that a loop was provided at this station for southbound trains. The signal in the 'off' position denotes that the train has a clear road through the main platform line. A new signal box was opened at Groombridge in November 1958 when the station area was resignalled. The new structure proved to be something of a white elephant, and lasted barely ten years. It closed in January 1969 when the Ashurst spur was taken out of use. *Paul Leavens*

Class L1 4-4-0 No.31756 sprints along with the 9am Brighton to Tonbridge train, which was photographed between Groombridge and Tunbridge Wells West in September 1959. The train is a set of four Maunsell Restriction 1 coaches. These were narrow-bodied, flat-sided vehicles which were specially built for lines with restricted clearances, such as Grove tunnel, which was situated between Tunbridge Wells West and Central stations. The L1 Class engines were introduced in 1926, as a development of the SE&CR L Class. Fifteen locomotives were constructed by the North British Locomotive Co. of Glasgow, primarily for use on Folkestone expresses. They differed from the 1914-built L Class by having smaller cylinders, higher boiler pressure, a higher running plate and an improved cab. They were the final design of inside cylinder 4-4-0 in Great Britain and proved very successful, before loads increased. The last survivor was withdrawn in 1962. *Paul Leavens*

Above: Sixty-six Class H 0-4-4T locomotives were built between 1904 and 1909 for suburban passenger use on the South Eastern and Chatham Railway. An interesting feature of the design was the 'Pagoda' cab which gave the crew additional protection. Following electrification of the Eastern Section suburban services in the 1920s, the H Class migrated to the country depots for use on secondary and branch line passenger services, to which they were ideally suited. In this view No.31544 is seen propelling a Tunbridge Wells West to Oxted train near Groombridge in July 1961. The last representatives of the H Class survived in this area until early 1964. *C. Hogg*

Right: BR Standard Class 4MT No.80145 heads a Brighton to Tonbridge train near Groombridge on 1st July 1961. The location is Adams Well crossing, the crossing keeper's cottage being visible towards the rear of the train. After leaving Groombridge the line to Tunbridge Wells runs parallel to the county boundary with Kent for about two miles before crossing into Kent near the site of the former High Rocks Halt. It is likely that the fields on the right, which are partially visible between the trees, are on the other side of a tributary of the River Medway, which forms the boundary. *C. Hogg*

Left: The BR Standard Class 4MT 2-6-4Ts were a familiar sight in Sussex from their introduction in 1951 until the end of regular steam traction in the county in 1965. They were particularly common in East Sussex on services from Tunbridge Wells to Brighton, Eastbourne and London (via Oxted), although the latter is strictly speaking outside the scope of this volume as it ran for only a short distance in Sussex. The train depicted here, the 1.47pm from Tunbridge Wells West to Victoria, is in the latter category. It is seen near Groombridge with No.80017 in charge on 1st July 1961. Like the locomotive, the coaches are also of BR Standard design. *C. Hogg*

Right: This Brighton to Tonbridge train, hauled by D1 Class 4-4-0 No.31487, is seen just north of the site of High Rocks Halt, between Groombridge and Tunbridge Wells West in September 1959. Twenty-one members of this class were rebuilt by Maunsell from SE&CR D Class engines between 1921 and 1927. As rebuilt, despite their modest dimensions and weight, they were excellent engines and performed regularly on certain Kent Coast services until electrification, after which they worked out their days on less exacting duties. All were gone by the end of 1961. The border between East Sussex and Kent crosses the railway at this point, and maybe only part of the train is actually in Sussex. When the author visited the location in February 1997, the concrete permanent way hut was still in evidence, but, not surprisingly, the attractive 'whistle' sign was no more. High Rocks Halt took its name from a picturesque outcrop of sandstone rock, which was situated atop a woodland ridge in the adjacent Broadwater forest. The halt, a wooden structure, was opened in 1907 for the pleasure traffic, but became an early closure casualty from 5th May 1952, after a temporary wartime closure from October 1939 to June 1942.
Paul Leavens

An unidentified Maunsell 'Mogul' leaves Hailsham, on the Tunbridge Wells to Eastbourne 'Cuckoo' line, with a train to Eastbourne in the early 1960s. There were some short workings between Eastbourne and Hailsham and it is likely that this train is one of these. Hailsham first appeared on the railway map in 1849 when a branch line from Polegate was opened: it even boasted a small engine shed for a time, but this was demolished in 1892. The Hailsham to Tunbridge Wells section was opened throughout on 1st September 1880 and closed, as far as Eridge, in June 1965 as a result of the Beeching axe. The section southwards from Hailsham to Polegate remained open for a further three years, closing in September 1968. *G. Daniels*

Above: On 11th June 1965, the 3.14pm Tunbridge Wells West to Eastbourne train was photographed as it was about to enter Argos Hill tunnel, between Rotherfield and Mayfield. Motive power is provided by BR Standard Class 4MT tank locomotive No.80142. Argos Hill was the highest point reached on the line and, apart from a steep climb into Heathfield, the crew of No.80142 will be able to take it relatively easily for the rest of the journey to the coast. Perhaps it should be noted, however, that a three-coach train was hardly a taxing load for one of these engines. *J. J. Smith*

Right: The 'Cuckoo Line' was probably the most scenic of all Sussex branch railways, providing one of the most pleasant and relaxing journeys one could wish for. It traversed some delightful Wealden countryside, as exemplified here in this picture of the 4.45pm from Eastbourne to Tunbridge Wells heading north near Mayfield on 11th June 1965. *J. J. Smith*

THE HASTINGS LINE

A motor train to Bexhill West headed by an SE&CR H Class 0-4-4T sits in the down bay at Crowhurst in April 1958, doubtless awaiting the arrival of a main line train from London. Construction of the short 4½ mile long branch to Bexhill was sanctioned in 1897, but the terrain presented major difficulties – deep cuttings and long embankments being required, in addition to a seventeen-arch viaduct across the Combe Haven valley. As a result of these problems, the line took over four years to complete, and it eventually opened for traffic on 1st June 1902. The line was built by a local company, nominally independent of the SE&CR. Despite the shorter distance from London by the SE&CR route (62 miles, compared to the LB&SCR's 72 miles long route), the SE&CR was never really able to challenge the supremacy of the 'Brighton' company, perhaps because the LB&SCR station was in a much more convenient position in the town centre. For many years, through London services were provided, but these declined before the Second World War, being replaced by push-pull sets which connected at Crowhurst, as seen here. The branch remained a sleepy backwater, and its fortunes failed to be revived by diesel units which were introduced in 1958. Following further years of decline, the line was closed in June 1964. The push-pull set is unusual in having been converted from ex-SE&CR coaches, part of a standard 3-coach 'Birdcage' set. *C. Hogg/Colour-Rail*

The 2.56pm Hastings to Tonbridge stopping train is pictured leaving Wadhurst on a sunny June day in 1957: 'Schools' Class 4-4-0 No.30909 *St Paul's*, in BR lined black livery, is the motive power. The train is formed of a SE&CR 'Birdcage' set of coaches in red livery – hardly a taxing load for such a powerful locomotive. Wadhurst station marks the summit of a nine-mile climb, most of it at 1 in 100 or thereabouts, from a point just beyond Robertsbridge. In the opposite direction, the climb approaching Wadhurst is less severe, but there is a long uphill section from Tonbridge to near Frant. *St Paul's* was built at Eastleigh Works in July 1930. It worked initially from Eastbourne shed on trains to London, but following the lifting of gauging and weight restrictions on the Hastings Line, *St Paul's* became one of the first members of its class to work on that route, on 6th July 1931. So, the long association of the class with the Hastings Line had begun, with many of the class, including *St Paul's*, being based at St Leonards. No.30909, however, worked from other sheds during its career, in addition to St Leonards, including Stewarts Lane and Ramsgate, and towards the end of its working life operated, most unusually, from Guildford. It was taken out of traffic in February 1962. *C. Hogg/Colour-Rail*

L1 Class 4-4-0 No.31783 is seen shortly after leaving West St Leonards with the 7.25pm Hastings to Charing Cross train on 16th June 1957. The train is formed of the unique 9-car set No.389, which is composed entirely of ex-SE&CR corridor vehicles, including former tri-composite brakes at either end. This was the final day of all-steam operation on this line prior to the introduction of the first batch of 6-car diesel units the following day. Many of St Leonards depot's 'Schools' Class engines were then transferred away, mainly to London area sheds such as Nine Elms and Stewarts Lane. Almost exactly a year later a second batch of diesel units resulted in the closure of St Leonards depot, and passenger steam working over the Hastings line became a thing of the past. *N. W. Sprinks*

The 'Schools' Class 4-4-0s are generally considered to be Maunsell's most successful locomotive type, their compact design giving an impression of power and speed, both of which characteristics they possessed in abundance. They were designed principally for the limited clearances and steep gradients of the Tonbridge to Hastings line, although they initially worked on the Western Section. In mid-1931, they were cleared for working the Hastings line, and it was here where some of their finest work was achieved. In this picture, 'Schools' Class locomotive No.30920, *Rugby* is seen tackling the tightly-curved 1 in 100 climb away from West St Leonards with the 6.35pm Hastings to Charing Cross train, on 16th June 1957. Despite the heavy ten-coach train the locomotive appears to be blowing-off, providing ample testament to the prodigious haulage capacity of these engines. *N. W. Sprinks*

In June 1957, the 10.38am train from Tonbridge to Hastings is seen leaving Frant behind L Class 4-4-0 No.31760, amidst some glorious scenery so typical of this part of the Sussex Weald. The first coach behind the locomotive is a distinctive vehicle which was designed by the SE&CR primarily for use on Continental boat trains from London to Dover and Folkestone. They were commonly known as 'matchboard' coaches because of the unusual vertical panelling below the waist. The other vehicles appear to be Southern Railway narrow-bodied carriages, which were specially designed for the limited clearances of tunnels on the line *N. W. Sprinks*

Maunsell 'Schools' Class 4-4-0 No.30929, *Malvern*, was pictured between Tunbridge Wells Central and Frant hauling the 9.25am Charing Cross to Hastings train in June 1957. The Sussex county boundary with Kent runs across the top of Strawberry Hill Tunnel, the position of which is indicated by the smoke in the background, so this photograph only just qualifies for inclusion in this album. *Malvern* was built at Eastleigh Works in July 1934, and during its career was based at Fratton, Bournemouth and Brighton in addition to various sheds on the South Eastern Section. It was amongst the final batch of 'Schools' class engines which were withdrawn at the end of 1962. *N. W. Sprinks*

LB&SCR 'Terrier' 0-6-0T No.32670 awaits the arrival of a LCGB rail tour, the 'South Eastern Limited', at Robertsbridge on 11th June 1961. The other 'Terrier', which is partially visible, is No.32662. The two 0-6-0Ts were waiting to take the train along the Kent and East Sussex line to Tenterden. The rail tour was run to mark the end of main line steam traction in Kent, which was due to be eliminated from the following day, when the London-Tonbridge-Dover main line and Paddock Wood to Maidstone West branch were electrified. The tour also provided an opportunity for a final run over the Hawkhurst branch and the K&ESR line, both of which were closed completely from 12th June 1961. The K&ESR line was a truly rural one, and during the journey quick sighted participants were able to see a startled fox dashing across a cornfield, near Junction Road halt. *N. W. Sprinks*

THE KENT & EAST SUSSEX LINE

Throughout this book, it has been the author's objective to portray everyday scenes on the railways of Sussex, when steam traction was still supreme. Photographs of railtours have, therefore, been generally avoided, except when they have depicted a locomotive type or stretch of line which would have otherwise not been included. This gem of a picture was taken on the Kent and East Sussex Line. It shows a Branch Line Society railtour returning from Tenterden to Robertsbridge on 12th April 1958. The train is seen between Bodiam and Junction Road, passing hop fields which could give the misleading impression that the picture was taken in Kent, but this view is actually in Sussex, the county border being more than two miles distant. The formation consists of four Maunsell 'Restriction 0' (Hastings Line gauge) coaches powered by a LB&SCR 'Terrier' at each end of the train. The locomotives are Nos. 32636, at the head of the train, and 32678 at the rear. This was the usual method for operation of special passenger trains during the twilight years of the K&ESR section. Regular passenger services on the line ceased in 1954, and prior to that event passenger accommodation had normally been provided by a ramshackle pre-grouping vehicle usually attached to a mixed train. *N. W. Sprinks*